GREAT BLACK SWAMP
Woods & Wanders:
NATURE'S JEWELS IN NORTHWEST OHIO

BY JIM MOLLENKOPF

Lake of the Cat Publishing
P.O. Box 351454
Toledo, OH 43635-1454

Book Design by: William Pritchard

ISBN 0-9665910-451995

LCCN 2004098608

TABLE OF CONTENTS

FOREWORD

"WHERE IS THE EAGLE? GONE."

SO WROTE SUQUAMISH INDIAN CHIEF SEATTLE IN A LETTER TO
PRESIDENT FRANKLIN PIERCE IN 1855 AS WHITE SETTLERS WERE OVER-
WHELMING HIS LAND. "THERE IS NO QUIET PLACE IN THE WHITE MAN'S
CITIES," HE ALSO OBSERVED. "NO PLACE TO HEAR THE LEAVES OF SPRING
OR THE RUSTLE OF INSECT WINGS. AND WHAT IS THERE TO LIFE IF A MAN
CANNOT HEAR THE LOVELY CRY OF THE WHIPPOORWILL OR THE ARGU-
MENTS OF THE FROG AROUND THE POND AT NIGHT."

Although the saddened old chief was referring to the changes to the
land in the Great Northwest, he could have been describing northwest
Ohio. Here also the arrival of settlers meant vast and permanent changes
to the land. Tall forests were felled, rivers and lakes were dirtied, and the
Great Black Swamp was drained into memory. Virtually gone too, for a
time, was the eagle.

But not every wild or open place was taken. Parks, wildlife refuges,
and nature preserves—local, state, and federal—were saved by people of
vision over the years and there are many places in northwest Ohio where
nature and its beauty can be found, where the rustle of insect wings and
the arguments of the frogs can still be heard, places where even a majestic
bald eagle can be seen on wing.

This book presents a selection of these places—places that are open
to everyone. It includes wetlands and woods, rivers and streams, lakes

and ponds, and gardens and estuaries. It is not, nor was it meant to be, a comprehensive catalogue of all the natural areas found in northwest Ohio.

This book is dedicated to my late nephew Dan Schipper of Morristown, New Jersey who overcame his first bout with cancer but was overwhelmed by his second. Blessed with ability, he expressed his creativity through art, music, and poetry, a light too soon darkened. Through the course of his illnesses he bore his burdens with dignity, grace, and a concern for the feelings and well being of others. He was, in the end, a teacher.

"I can remember the scent of crackling wood, melting deep within the fire. Deep within the woods, under the moonlight of a Canadian sky. The warmth of the fire swarms around me. The thick clouds of smoke, from the burning embers, tickle the inside of my nose. And this cloud condenses as it slips down through my throat. And I see it, feel it, smell the warmth as it lifts up my body, floating off through the trees. This is the scent I hold so sacred, that whenever I'm afraid, or left alone, I can remember the smell of those glowing embers from the camp fire. One of my escapes. With those memories of that delicious scent, I'll go back in time where I feel safe. Safe under that brisk Canadian moonlight."

Smell, by Dan Schipper
August 14, 1984–December 15, 2002

GREAT BLACK SWAMP

Woods & Wanders:

NATURE'S JEWELS IN NORTHWEST OHIO

CHAPTER I

ONE OF THE LAST GREAT PLACES: THE OAK OPENINGS

N̄EARLY TWO HUNDRED YEARS AGO, SETTLERS GOING WEST MADE AN ARDUOUS JOURNEY THROUGH WOODS AND WILDS OF NORTHERN AND NORTHWESTERN OHIO, WHICH IN-CLUDED SLOGGING THROUGH THE GREAT BLACK SWAMP. IN WHAT IS TODAY WESTERN LUCAS COUNTY, A SURPRISE AWAITED THEM. FOR HERE WAS NOT THICK FOREST OR DENSE SWAMP BUT SANDY PLAINS, DOTTED WITH SCATTERED OAK TREES AND REMARKABLY FREE OF UNDERBRUSH, WHERE A WAGON COULD BE PULLED IN MOST ANY DIRECTION WITHOUT HACKING A PATH. THE SETTLERS LOOKED AT THIS LAND AND CALLED IT THE OAK OPENINGS.

The unique terrain of the Oak Openings had its genesis around 13,000 years ago in a series of lakes that covered the region, the legacy left by the last glaciers to pass over northwest Ohio. Although the lakes are long gone their beaches remain, four ancient ones running through Lucas, Fulton and Henry Counties. For thousands of years these sandy environments were home to oak savannas and treeless wet prairies, communities that were combinations of the forests of the east and the prairies of the west. High water tables sustained the wet prairies while dry, sandy soil and wildfires maintained the oak savanna environment.

The sun filters through the mist on a spring morning at Irwin Prairie.

The settlement of the area changed all this. Wildfires were controlled and water tables were lowered by the digging of drainage ditches. Wet prairies sprouted into woods and the suppression of fire led to considerable woody undergrowth in the once open oak savannas. In addition, much of the land was converted to agriculture.

However, efforts have been ongoing since the 1930s to both conserve and to return lands in the Oak Openings region to their original condition. The Metroparks of the Toledo Area has several parks in the region, the largest being the nearly 3,700–acre Oak Openings Preserve. The Ohio Department of Natural Resources maintains several areas, including Irwin Prairie State Nature Preserve. Even the private, non-profit sector is involved with The Nature Conservancy owning and operating the 575–acre Kitty Todd Preserve.

Due to these efforts, which are ongoing, the Oak Openings is one of North America's most unique and diverse areas, an area where high quality oak savanna and wet prairie communities can still be found. Home to 180 globally rare forms of plant and animal life, researchers come from all over the country to study its environs. Although domain that is the Oak Openings might lack the dramatic appeal of a cascading waterfall or an old growth forest, it is no less important.

IRWIN PRAIRIE STATE NATURE PRESERVE

The word "prairie" conjures up visual images of a plain or meadow or some other open expanse, perhaps with tall grass waving in the wind. The word may even evoke the historical image of a covered wagon being pulled by a team of oxen, clouds of dust billowing in its wake.

At Irwin Prairie State Nature Preserve in western Lucas County there is a different sort of prairie, one no covered wagon was pulled across, at least not without considerable difficulty. For the land contained there is classified as a wet prairie, one

Late summer finds wildflowers, including swamp marigolds, flourishing at Irwin Prairie.

where the groundwater is at or above ground level most of the year, and is one of the few remaining examples of such in the state.

Even though it spreads over 180–plus acres, Irwin Prairie is one of those places that can be easily missed. Its entrance is marked by a small parking lot and sign along Bancroft Street, one that could be driven past almost in a blink of an eye. From that small parking lot, however, a narrow boardwalk departs and takes the visitor into an interesting world, one that has been altered little since the first settlers came to the area.

The boardwalk leaves to the south and passes through areas of pin oak and shrub swamp, two of the distinct "communities" of Irwin Prairie. The walk then turns sharply to the east and crosses Irwin Road where a large, wet sedge meadow community awaits. Here the dominant plant, twig-rush, is a close relative of the saw grass of Florida Everglades fame. A state brochure describes this sedge meadow as the "finest remaining sedge meadow" in all of Ohio, which gives an idea of the value of Irwin Prairie.

Through the broad, flat sedge meadow the walk continues, a concert of frogs resounding during the wet season. The land then rises ever so slightly and dries a bit, and the walk enters another pin oak community, denser than the first. In this thick stand, the boardwalk circles off in two directions to form a loop. It ends at what for the first-time visitor is a bit of serendipity—a broad grass meadow or marsh, one that is actually a shallow lake during the wet months. Here an elevated platform provides a fine view of this wetland, a sea of green rising out of shimmering water and waving in the breeze on a summer's day.

In addition, Irwin Prairie is home to an array of plants, some of them very rare and some of which are no longer found anywhere else in the state of Ohio. In July and August, wildflowers brighten the prairie and mosquito repellent is recommended. The prairie also provides good birdwatching opportunities, particularly during spring migration when the uncommonly seen blue-winged warbler and its rarely seen hybrid, the Brewster's warbler, are annual visitors.

Pink trillium grows along Irwin Prairie's boardwalk in early summer.

Kitty Todd Preserve

Rich and Rare Were the Gems She Wore is the title of a poem by the Irish poet Thomas Moore. Rich and rare describe the natural gems worn by the Kitty Todd Preserve in western Lucas County, home to more rare species than any other area of the state of Ohio. Over 90 species of plants and 20 species of animals considered to be rare by the state find a home in Kitty Todd's 620 acres. Originally known as the Schwamberger Prairie and since named for an early conservationist in the area, the preserve is owned and operated by The Nature Conservancy. The group's mission—"Saving the Last Great Places on Earth"—is evident here.

A community of rare plants and animals find haven here in a world that increasingly crowds them out. Badgers, the endangered lark sparrow, the rare spotted turtle and the federally protected Karner blue butterfly secure refuge here where the wild lupine grows, the delicate flower being the Karner blue's sole larval food source. The tiny butterfly fluttering over the lavender lupine is a spectacle in azure. Some of the other plants found here include little bluestem, orange-fringed orchid, yellow false indigo, western sunflower, and grass pink orchid—their very names form a verbal rainbow.

From a small parking lot, the 0.4–mile Oak Savanna Trail winds along dry sandy ground before linking with the Cactus Loop Trail of about the same length. Both trails are pleasant gambols through scattered oaks and open prairies, land that is little changed by mankind.

The open oaks of the savanna make for relatively easy viewing of the rare lark sparrow, as well as more common and colorful species such as the red-headed woodpecker,

The sandy soil of Kitty Todd Nature Preserve supports a wide variety of rare plant and animal species. Wild lupine is the sole larval food source for the federally endangered karner blue butterfly.

common yellowthroat warbler, Baltimore oriole, and eastern towhee. In late May and June stands of violet lupine light up the ground, at times even brighter when the backdrop is a windblown sand dune.

Kitty Todd Preserve is located at 10420 Old State Line Road in western Lucas County, about one mile north of Toledo Express Airport. Hours are 9 A.M. to 5 P.M. Monday through Friday and the first full weekend of the month May through October only. There is a small parking area with informational displays and an Oak Openings Native Display Garden, no other facilities. For more information on guided walks or preserve volunteer projects call 419–867–1521.

OAK OPENINGS PRESERVE METROPARK

By far the largest protected tract of Oak Openings soil lies within the Metroparks of the Toledo Area parcel of the same name. The nearly 3,700–acre preserve, which is the largest of the Metroparks' holdings, provides habitat for a range of plant and animal life, including threatened and endangered species—over 1,000 species of plants alone have been documented here. In addition, trails for all seasons wander about Oak Openings. Upwards of forty miles of walking, hiking, biking, and skiing trails combined with twenty-three miles of horse trails and fifty miles of unmarked fire lanes provide ample opportunity to give the park and its lakes, woods, wetlands, and sand dunes a thorough scouring.

For those not looking to wear out a pair of walking shoes, the Sand Dunes Trail provides the opportunity to easily sample some of the exceptional habitats Oak Openings has to offer. The 1.7–mile Sand Dunes Trail (red) leaves the parking lot at the Buehner Walking Center and begins by passing through a stand of maple trees, the air scented at times by tall white and red pines. The maple trees come to an end almost abruptly and an oak savanna spreads before the eyes. Here scattered, muscular oak trees rise from a sandy plain. The floor of the plain is thick with ferns.

A bit further on, the trail leaves the oak savanna and climbs a bit and travels along the eastern edge of the Girdham Road Sand Dune, the largest of the open

Ferns carpet the oak savanna floor along the Sand Dunes Trail in Oak Openings.

sand dunes within the preserve. The journey along the border of the dune is a stroll through remarkable contrast. Immediately to the east is a tall, shady, and darkened forest, while on the west are large, open areas of sand glowing in the sun, and punctuated in places by small trees and shrubby growth. Ancient glacial lakes deposited the sand here millennia ago and it remains today as one of the most unique environments in northwest Ohio. Although the sand of the dune might be extremely old, that doesn't mean it's at rest. The wind-whipped dune is on the move to the east, ever so slightly, covering and smothering vegetation as it goes.

The trail curls away from the dune and returns to the woods, maple at first then mixed hardwood, then oak savanna and eventually back to the trailhead and Buehner Walking Center.

Oak Openings Preserve is located in southwestern Lucas County, and can be reached from State Route 295, Girdham Road or State Route 64 going south from Airport Highway, just west of Toledo Express Airport. The park is open 7 A.M. to dark year-round. For more information call the park at 419–826–6463.

SECOR METROPARK

With habitats ranging from tallgrass prairie to woodland pond to tall woods, it's a bit surprising to learn that the existence of Secor Metropark is rooted in an old, downtown Toledo parking lot. In 1941, Arthur J. Secor donated a small parking lot to the park system in memory of his parents and the income generated from its operation led to the purchase of the park's land in 1953.

Around 6.5 miles of walking trails and 3.4 miles of all-purpose trails travel about Secor, which at 600 acres is the second largest of the Metroparks. Its most unique environment may be a restored prairie and the aptly named Prairie Trail (orange) takes you there. Unlike the wet prairie a stone's throw away at Irwin Prairie, this is a dry one. The easy 0.6–mile mowed grass trail is perhaps best experienced near summer's end when growth in the prairie is abundant.

A deer peers through the woods along the Sand Dunes Trail in Oak Openings.

On a fine September day the grass of the prairie is thick and head high and colored in late summer amber. It waves ever so slightly in the breeze as wildflowers poke their head from the flaxen scene. The deep purples of New England aster and prairie blazing star are balanced by the delicate pink-violet of the daisy fleabane, the latter being busily worked by bumblebees and honeybees. Stands of goldenrod and the bright yellow blooms of prairie dock are here as well, while a few sprouts of Queen Anne's lace remain in mid-summer form. The sun is near its autumnal equinox and its rays are softer as it sojourns to the south while the shadows it casts stretch longer.

A shagbark hickory tree lords over the prairie and every now and again a crash through the branches signals that another hickory nut with its green, thick hull has tumbled to the ground, much to the gratitude of the squirrels. It's a harvest in progress. Another sound, much softer, is the calling of crickets. Their whirring, emanating throughout the prairie, is a reassuring resonance, one that says all is well with Mother Nature here.

Goldfinches, their color in early autumn fading, dash about gathering seeds while overhead a turkey vulture lingers on currents of air. Its great span of two-toned wings sweep a shadow over the tall grass as it glides in its customary rocking and tilting style. The vulture is slowly working its way south and will be long gone when winter lays a blanket of white over this prairie.

Another short walk, the 0.3–mile Woodland Pond Trail (blue), travels through a much different environment. The trail begins, passing by a black walnut tree with its handsome, deeply furrowed bark, a tree whose leaves fall before its fruit. The round, green-shelled walnuts hanging from the bare branches look like Christmas ornaments.

More green awaits beyond the walnut tree at the small woodland pond, the surface of which is dressed in a bright sheen of aquatic growth. From the observation deck the pond appears at first to be a study in stillness. But a swish in the water here and a swirl there tell of life going on underneath. The crack of a stick being stepped on leads to more activity as frogs make a hasty departure from the pond's

Grassy paths wind through a restored tallgrass prairie at Secor Park.

edge into the water. They plop softly through the green surface and disappear to safety below.

The tall trees on the banks of the pond paint its emerald surface in dark shadows while dead branches and logs protrude from the water here and there. From the observation deck the trail traces the east side of the pond under a canopy of towering tuliptrees and oak trees of old growth dimension. Thick trunks rise high in the air forty or more feet before the first branches sprout and virtually no sunlight reaches the black and damp soil here in remarkable contrast to the prairie only a short distance away. The short trail curls through the woods and back to the trailhead.

Back at the main parking lot are two points of interest—one modern, one historic. In 2003 the National Center for Nature Photography opened its doors, displaying the finest in national, regional, and local nature photography. Outstanding photographs are on display in both permanent collections and special exhibits. The center, which is a teaching facility as well, is said to be the only one of its kind in the country.

Just south of the parking lot several massive white oak trees stand well over a hundred years old and mighty in every sense of the word. They front Wolfinger Cemetery, a small burial ground that dates to 1835, one of the older cemeteries in northwest Ohio and probably one of the few cemeteries anywhere surrounded by a public park. On a knoll in the cemetery, a plaque on a boulder tells of the first white burial in the area.

Secor Metropark is located about six miles west of Toledo on U.S. 20 (Central Avenue) and is open daily 7 A.M. to dark. A total of six walking trails, ranging from 0.3 to 1.3 miles, wind throughout the park in addition to a 3.4-mile all-purpose trail. For more information call the park at 419–829–2761. The National Center for Nature Photography is open noon to 5 P.M. Saturdays and Sundays as well as Memorial Day, July 4, and Labor Day. For more information call the center at 419–829–6866.

The extensive sand dunes of Oak Openings are the remnant of glacial lakes that

This wall mural hangs from the National Center for Nature Photography located at Secor Park.

Crabapple trees heavy with fruit grow along the Prairie Trail at Secor Park.

CHAPTER II

OLD WOMAN CREEK ESTUARY

*A*LONG THE WATERS OF THE CREEK HERE A NUMBER OF YEARS BEFORE THE AMERICAN REVOLUTION, A YOUNG INDIAN MAIDEN WATCHED IN HORROR AS MEMBERS OF HER TRIBE PREPARED TO EXECUTE HER LOVER, A FRENCH EXPLORER. AT THE LAST INSTANT SHE FLUNG HERSELF IN FRONT OF HIM AND THEY WERE STRUCK BY THE SAME ARROW AND KILLED, TOGETHER FOREVER IN DEATH. HER AGING MOTHER, WRACKED WITH GRIEF, FLUNG HERSELF INTO THE WATERS OF THE CREEK AND DROWNED, THUS OLD WOMAN CREEK.

Whether or not this actually happened is anyone's guess. But that's how the legend goes and it makes a good story. The story here now is that one of Ohio's best remaining examples of natural estuary is preserved, protected and thriving. The conventional definition of an estuary is a place where inland fresh waters mingle with those of a salty sea to form a third type of water. However, the same phenomenon can occur in a freshwater-only situation. Here, for example, the waters of Old Woman Creek and Lake Erie combine to form a third type of water chemically different from either the creek or the lake.

Old Woman Creek Estuary is both a state nature preserve and a national estuarine research reserve, the only such one in the Great Lakes Biogeographic Region. To scientists and researchers it's a

*O*ld Woman Creek carves a path through the sand where it empties into Lake Erie.

laboratory for estuary study. To the nature aficionado it's over 500 acres of water, marshland, mature woods, and barrier beach. Over forty kinds of fish take advantage of its waters and over 300 species of both migratory and resident birds have been documented here. One of those residents is the bald eagle. A pair has been nesting here a number of years in a row.

From the visitor center parking lot a short, paved trail cuts across a hillside through dense woods. The trail emerges from the woods to an observation deck where the broad, open estuary almost leaps into view. Hundreds of yards wide, its lazy brown waters are dotted with beds of water lotus that stretch to tall marsh grasses on the far side.

From the deck might be spotted the Old Woman Creek's most famed resident, the bald eagle, as it flies over the waters of the estuary in search for food. "Avian Jumbo Jets," the informational display at the deck calls them. And if one happens by there's a pair of high-powered binoculars mounted on a stand with which to view them up close.

From the observation deck a graveled trail travels back along a hillside a bit through thick woods and the walker has the option of looping back to the visitor center or taking the mile-long Wintasta Trail. This trail, some of which is boardwalk and stairs, winds through both lowland and upland, shaded by a mature hardwood forest dominated by oak and hickory trees. It emerges into former farm fields that are gradually returning to the wild, then back to the visitor center and parking lot.

About a quarter mile west from the main part of the estuary on U.S. 6, a small parking area just over the bridge provides access to a barrier beach that separates the estuary from Lake Erie. Here the waters of Old Woman Creek have carved a path through the sand on their journey to the lake. The wind-swept barrier beach is an ongoing sculpture chiseled by wind and wave.

Old Woman Creek Estuary is located on U.S. 6 (Cleveland Road East) just east of Huron, and is open daily from 8 A.M. *until 5* P.M. **The visitor center is open Wednesday through Sunday from 1 to 5** P.M. **For more information call 419–433–4601.**

CHAPTER III

BLACK SWAMP WOODS

*A*LTHOUGH THE OVERWHELMING MAJORITY OF ORIGINAL BLACK SWAMP FOREST LONG AGO FELL VICTIM TO THE WOODCUTTER'S SAW THERE ARE A FEW STANDS REMAINING, INCLUDING ONE IN LUCAS COUNTY AND ANOTHER ONE IN WOOD COUNTY.

PEARSON METROPARK

For thousands of years much of northwest Ohio lay covered by a vast, luxuriant marsh. According to early observers parts of it were watery meadows of grass, veritable seas of living, moving, green that would undulate beautifully in a summer breeze. Other parts of it were low, thick, impenetrable brush and wild growth. Still other parts of it were majestic and untouched forests, cathedra-lesque stands of oak, sycamore, elm and hickory trees that soared skyward and blocked out the sun. Its thousands of square acres spread over all or parts of twelve counties stretching east to west from near Sandusky, Ohio to near Fort Wayne, Indiana and north to south from the Maumee River valley to near Findlay, Ohio.

Despite its raw beauty the marsh held, for the most part, no allure for humans. Early westward settlers who traveled through it saw its rich, black soil, inky waters and light-shuttering stands of

Water pools on the forest floor along the Wood Thrush Trail in Pearson Park.

trees, named it the Black Swamp and kept going. For the swamp also featured waist-high waters in the spring, voracious clouds of mosquitoes in the summer, and malarial fevers that started in late summer and lasted well into fall. Winter froze the swamp into an icy and isolated wilderness. It was a foreboding-looking place to those seeking land to clear and crops to plant and most wanted nothing to do with it. One man who traveled through it in 1815 wrote to his wife, "my great terrour, the Black Swamp, is passed."

Flash forward 100 years. Most of the Black Swamp is now gone; its waters drained, its wild growth cleared and its forests felled. But a small portion of forest remained just east of Toledo in the city of Oregon. It was about that time that East Toledo resident and reporter for *The Blade,* George W. Pearson, began a campaign to save the land, then known as the Bank Lands because the property was often mortgaged and held by banks as loan collateral. Over the years many others joined him in his efforts. However, it was George Pearson, who came to be known as "the first citizen of East Toledo" because of his strong loyalty and commitment to that part of the city, who was the sustaining force.

It would take twenty years, but on August 30, 1934 the land was dedicated as Pearson Park, named after George. Much of the park's 320 acres is original Black Swamp woodland and over the years it has become one of the most heavily visited of the Metroparks of the Toledo Area. Two 1.3–mile hiking trails, the Wood Thrush and the Black Swamp trails, wander through Pearson's aged woods. The Wood Thrush Trail meanders through both forest and open areas of Pearson while the Black Swamp Trail is strictly a walk in the woods.

A warm, mid-summer morning finds the woods especially humid after a dawn thunderstorm. Water, both from rainfall and the area's natural high water table, is pooled in places under the lofty canopy of timber above. The pools serve as reflecting ponds and the surrounding landscape is mirrored on their motionless surfaces. A slight breeze stirs, sending drops of rain sliding off the leaves of the tall

A gazebo provides a place to rest along the Black Swamp Trail in Pearson Park.

hardwoods, and splashing sounds echo through the forest. Another sound, the hum of the mosquito, abounds as well, a tune so familiar to Black Swamp settlers.

Many a settler family slogged through these woods in summer, their only protection from mosquitoes being thick clothing, head coverings and mittens. Perspiring profusely and drinking what water they could find, some must have stopped, leaned against a tree and wondered why they ever left home in the first place. They probably couldn't have imagined that these woods would one day be a recreational destination.

Around the circumference of the park is a nearly three-mile exercise trail with a surface of finely screened stone—a Black Swamp traveler would have loved to have had a surface like that to journey on. Paralleling much of the exercise trail is a three-mile bicycle trail which travels by a small lake that offers pedal boating in the summer and ice skating in the winter.

Near the center of the park is the Packer-Hammersmith Center, which has a Window on Wildlife and informational and pictorial displays on the history of the Great Black Swamp. And across from the center is a small stone memorial to George Pearson, without whose vision, dedication and persistence this land would have likely been just another piece of Black Swamp land swept away by development.

In 2002 the Metroparks of the Toledo Area acquired 300–plus acres north of the current park which, when opened to the public, will nearly double the park's size. Somewhere George W. Pearson surely is smiling.

Pearson Metropark is located off Navarre Avenue, (State Route 2) in Oregon, Ohio just east of Toledo. Other recreational opportunities there include softball diamonds, tennis courts, fishing and a soccer field. For more information call the park at 419–691–3997.

ST. JOHN'S/WINTERGARDEN NATURE PRESERVE

From the one-time heart of the Great Black Swamp in the city of Bowling Green in Wood County stands another peek into the past, the Wintergarden/St. John's Nature

S pring brings new growth to the trees along Pearson Park's Black Swamp Trail.

Preserve. Eighty acres make up the preserve, which is a mix of forest, meadow, prairie and wetland, managed to reflect the original biological diversity of the area. Don't be thrown off by the recreational field and manicured lawn bowling court at the preserve's entrance: the old growth woods, wildflower meadows, prairie grasses and wetland of the preserve harken to a time when the only Americans roaming the area were Native ones.

From the Rotary Nature Center, about two miles of walking trails depart in loops varying in length from fifteen minutes to an hour. The two woodlands of the preserve, Wintergarden Woods and St. John's Woods, mark the western and eastern segments of the preserve respectively, with Bordner Meadow occupying the center. It was in the meadow portion of the preserve where Stephen St. John, an attorney and farmer from New York who came here in 1841, tended his row crops while his livestock roamed the woods now bearing his name.

The woods of the preserve are thick and the growth on the ground is lush. This is especially so during a summer of ample rainfall when the woods are cast in an emerald hue of remarkable intensity. The trails meander through a mixed hardwood forest including huge oak trees slanting toward the sky. A few giant fallen oaks are here and there. Laying in damp decay on a hushed and darkened forest floor, it's a scene and a scent more reminiscent of northern Michigan woods than northwest Ohio ones.

In Bordner Meadow, native wildflowers bloom and the grasses grow tall. The thick woods, open meadow and wet areas of the preserve give a pretty good idea of the varying topography settlers encountered in traveling through the Great Black Swamp.

Wintergarden/St. John's Nature Preserve, located on Wintergarden Road on the southwestern edge of the city of Bowling Green, is open daily until dark. The Rotary Nature Center has a window on wildlife and naturalist's office. For more information call the office at 419–353–0301.

The old growth woods of Wintergarden/St. John's features lush ground cover, dense understory and huge oak trees.

Wildflowers grow among the meadow grasses in the Bordner Meadow area of Wintergarden/St. John's Woods.

CHAPTER IV

THE EVERGLADES OF NORTHWEST OHIO

THE SHORELINES ADJACENT TO MOST GREAT LAKES CITIES ARE THICK WITH PRIVATE HOMES, CONDOS, MARINAS AND OTHER MAN-MADE DEVELOPMENTS THAT HAVE OBLITERATED THE ORIGINAL LANDSCAPE AND ARE OFF-LIMITS TO THE GENERAL PUBLIC. THE LAKE ERIE SHORE EAST OF TOLEDO DIFFERS GREATLY FROM THIS. HERE MANY THOUSANDS OF ACRES OF LAKESHORE AND WETLAND LAY IN THE PUBLIC DOMAIN IN STATE AND FEDERAL WILDLIFE REFUGES AND STATE PARKS. WHAT'S MORE IS THAT MUCH OF THE WETLAND IS PRISTINE, LITTLE CHANGED FROM THE DAYS WHEN ONLY NATIVE AMERICANS INHABITED THE LAND. IT IS ORIGINAL WILDERNESS IN AN AREA OF THE COUNTRY THAT HAS VERY LITTLE AND IN A PART OF THE STATE THAT HAS LOST NEARLY 98 PERCENT OF ITS WETLANDS TO URBAN DEVELOPMENT AND AGRICULTURE.

Marshes in the past were generally viewed as hostile places by humans: dark, bug-infested areas of stagnant water and wild growth that needed to be drained and plowed into submission before they could be of any practical use. Historically, Lake Erie's marshes were appreciated primarily by duck hunters who protected them in private preserves and clubs. Around the middle of the last century as the perception of marshes as places of value had become more mainstream,

*T*he rarest of the woodland warblers, the Kirtland's warbler, is likewise rarely seen during spring migration at Magee Marsh This particular bird lingered for a couple of days in 1997.

A morning sun lights the cottonwood trees and beach of Crane Creek State Park

the state and federal government began buying up these clubs and preserves, ensuring forever their protection. The Cedar Point Shooting Club is now part of history but its legacy lives on in the Cedar Point National Wildlife Refuge it helped preserve.

The Lake Erie marshes in northwest Ohio are but a fragmentary remnant of a once massive marsh, the Great Black Swamp, a rectangular-shaped plain roughly forty miles wide and 120 miles long that stretched from near Sandusky, Ohio to near Fort Wayne, Indiana and which was drained from existence by the end of the nineteenth century.

The Lake Erie marshes provide a superior haven to a wide variety of life, both plant and animal. For example, their habitats provide shelter to more birds, mammals and amphibians per acre than any other area in the state of Ohio. And many of the approximately 15,000 acres of marsh are, quite literally, for the birds, as access by humans is controlled and restricted to those with permits only.

The marshes can provide many treats for the eyes: the majesty of a bald eagle soaring overhead; the brilliant white of a great egret posing in the morning sun; the dignified bearing of a great blue heron standing utterly still while waiting for a fish to swim by; the magnificence of a great horned owl, sleeping high in a tree, who's thoroughly indifferent to those observing him from below; or the V-shaped rippling of water trailing behind a muskrat as he swims just below the marsh surface while making his rounds.

Although the Lake Erie marshes are home to wildlife year-round, spring migration is a special time as hundreds of species of birds can be seen as they stop and feed before continuing their journey beyond Lake Erie and on north. Songbirds, shorebirds, waterfowl and raptors surge through the marshes in great numbers, drawing birdwatchers from many parts of the country.

Most of the lakeshore marshland in the public domain lies along a roughly twenty-mile tract in western Ottawa and eastern Lucas counties stretching between Crane Creek State Park/Magee Marsh Wildlife Area and Maumee Bay State Park. Northwest Ohio is fortunate to have such extensive and accessible wetland.

Summer brings out the swamp rose mallow at Magee Marsh.

Crane Creek State Park and Magee Marsh Wildlife Area combine to provide what is perhaps the best the Lake Erie shore has to offer in northwest Ohio. Large tracts of wild marshland, spectacular birdwatching, an interpretive center, trails and observation decks, and an over half-mile long sandy swimming beach and picnic grounds shaded by tall cottonwoods await the visitor here. What make these areas special is the accessibility they offer to both motorists and walkers.

The entrance to Crane Creek and Magee Marsh leaves State Route 2 in western Ottawa County and those driving almost immediately enter another world. Along the nearly two-mile drive to Lake Erie stands the Sportsmen Migratory Bird Center, a handsome, rustic, two-story structure built in 1970. The exhibits inside include hundreds of birds mounted and displayed, ranging in size from the hummingbird to the bald eagle. There are also antique duck decoys and hunting rifles, marsh lore and information on the history of the area, and even a collection of a hundred different bird eggs collected between 1925 and 1930. Overlooking a pond adjacent to the bird center stands an observation tower and there's a walking trail that circles the pond while another winds through a nearby swamp forest.

Beyond the center the road heads straight north and opens up into a causeway with marshland stretching to the east and west almost as far as the eye can see—no other venue in northwest Ohio provides such extensive wetland viewing from the automobile.

Many species of waterfowl can be seen along here, including North America's largest waterfowl, the once nearly extinct trumpeter swan, several pair of which were introduced here in the late 1990s In the spring the roadside is a virtual maternity ward for Canada geese as parent geese shepherd along their broods of fuzzy, yellow goslings. The road reaches Lake Erie and feeds into an extensive parking area with the swimming beach and picnic ground of the state park on the lake side and the Magee Marsh Bird Trail on the other.

An autumn sun slips over the horizon at Magee Marsh Wildlife Area.

If area bird lovers could die and go to heaven, that heaven just might be the Magee Marsh Bird Trail. Winding through a forested beach ridge, the over half-mile boardwalk provides some of the best songbird watching in the Midwest during spring migration, which peaks during the first three weeks of May. At that time license plates from dozens of states and several Canadian provinces appear in the parking lots. In 2002, *Birders World* magazine listed Magee Marsh as one of the top ten birdwatching areas in North America, ranking it with such places as Everglades National Park in Florida and Point Pelee National Park in Ontario.

Birds fly north by the millions from their winter homes in Central and South America and the wild, swamp forest of the beach ridge and surrounding wetlands provide an excellent place to stop, rest and feed before making the flight over or around the open waters of Lake Erie. The songbirds seen along the trail at Magee Marsh include warblers—over thirty-five different species have been identified here. Buntings, tanagers, orioles, grosbeaks, vireos and flycatchers—all in breeding plumage—flock through as well, creating an annual rainbow of color.

The number of birds seen along the bird trail varies day-to-day during spring migration with weather being an important factor. Birds like to ride northward on south or southwesterly winds, and on days with such winds the birding is usually good. A strong warm front riding up from the south and passing over the lakeshore, particularly overnight when songbirds migrate, can drop thousands of new arrivals in the trees along the trail providing a spectacular day of birdwatching. On such "fallout" days the trail is alive with birds dashing from tree to tree feeding on insects, their songs filling the air. On such days two, three, and sometimes even four warblers can appear in the same binoculars' view. And on such days even veteran birders walk around with grins on their faces.

Conversely, north or northwesterly winds can diminish bird numbers although they sometimes have the effect of "grounding" the birds who build up in numbers while waiting for the wind to turn around and aid their flight over Lake Erie. One should keep in mind that when it comes to predicting the number of

A great egret poses near the access road at the Ottawa Refuge.

birds along the trail on a given day and the effect of weather on the same, there are, of course, no guarantees except for perhaps one: a stiff, raw, northeast wind off the chilly May waters of Lake Erie virtually promises a poor birding day.

By the end of May, most of the migratory birds have passed through, leaving Magee Marsh to resident species. Over 130 species have been found nesting here. Summer finds the marsh lush with vegetation, including water lilies, bur marigolds and the swamp rose mallow whose blooms brighten the landscape in July and August. In September, the migratory birds are returning south. But their return is spread out over a longer period of time. And with their colors faded to winter plumage and the trees along the bird trail thick with growth after a long, hot summer, it's nowhere near the spring show. Autumn fades into winter and the marsh becomes quiet until spring when the birds, and those who love to watch them, return.

Crane Creek State Park and Magee Marsh Wildlife Area, located on State Route 2 in western Ottawa County, are open year-round. The state park beach has picnic tables, grills, and changing booths. The Lake Erie waters off the park offer year-round fishing. For more information call the park at 419–898–2495. Magee Marsh's Sportsmen Migratory Bird Center is open 8 A.M. to 5 P.M. Monday through Friday, and 11 A.M. to 5 P.M. Saturday and Sunday, March through November with special hours of 8 A.M. to 5 P.M. on Saturday and Sunday in April and May during the migratory season. A number of events are held at the marsh on International Migratory Bird Day, which is celebrated annually the second weekend in May. The Magee Marsh Bird Trail is all boardwalk and handicapped accessible. For more information call the marsh at 419–898–0960.

OTTAWA NATIONAL WILDLIFE REFUGE

Adjoining the Crane Creek/Magee Marsh complex just to the west is the Ottawa National Wildlife Refuge, a sprawling wetland totalling over 4,600 acres established in 1961 when the U.S. Fish and Wildlife Service bought up a number of small, privately owned marshes. It has since added thousands of additional acres in four other locations, bringing the total acreage in the Ottawa National Wildlife Refuge to around 9,000, with more acres to be added in the future.

Ottawa is the only one of the five refuge areas that is open to the public without a permit. Four foot trails leaving from a small parking about a half-mile off of State

Water lotus brightens the Ottawa Refuge during the second half of summer.

Route 2 include a 0.25–mile loop and longer paths of 2.0, 3.1 and 4.5 miles. Most of the trails are of crushed gravel along level dikes. Auto tours, dependent on weather and road conditions, are allowed on a monthly basis April through December.

When it comes to managing habitat for wildlife, Ottawa is definitely a "hands-on" place. Dikes, ditches, pumps and other water control devices are used to regulate water levels in much of the refuge to produce the best marsh habitat possible. The diked bodies of water, or impoundments, are kept at differing depths to produce a variety of plant growth, thus meeting the feeding and resting needs of both resident and migratory waterfowl, songbirds and other wildlife. The resident wildlife here include once nearly extinct bald eagles which can be seen in flight— the areas near the nests of the federally protected birds are off limits to the public.

Located along the Mississippi and Atlantic flyways, tens of thousands of birds stop over at this important way station during their long, arduous journeys north in the spring and back south in the fall. Over 320 species have been recorded here; from the Acadian flycatcher to the yellow-crowned night heron. They stop, feed, and rest before heeding their ancestral call to move on in a rhythm as timeless as the ages.

The trails that journey along the dikes of the refuge take hikers to a tranquil world, one seldom seen, of varied wetlands, open waters, tallgrass prairie, and of dark woods that recall the refuge's Great Black Swamp days. It is a world unique and rare in northwest Ohio, where the reverie of watching a bald eagle soar high overhead can be broken by the honks of Canada geese, scolding for passing too close to their trailside brood.

The other holdings in the Ottawa National Wildlife Refuge complex are the Cedar Point Refuge on Maumee Bay; the West Sister Island Refuge nine miles off the Lake Erie shore; and the Darby and Navarre marshes in Ottawa County. Access to these refuges is by permit only. The Ottawa Refuge is open year-round and brochures and latrines are available at the parking lot. There is a small visitor center in the refuge office open 8 A.M. to 4 P.M. Monday through Friday. A new $1.9 million visitor center is scheduled for completion in 2006 The refuge provides educational programs for children and adults as well as cross-country skiing opportunities in the winter. For more information call the refuge at 419–898–0014.

Metzger Marsh as seen from the dike along Lake Erie.

A great blue heron crouches as it walks along an impoundment at the Ottawa Refuge.

West of Ottawa National Wildlife Refuge lies Metzger Marsh Wildlife Area, an over 500–acre wetland. Although its purpose is primarily that of a public hunting and fishing area, it also provides fine marshland viewing opportunities from both the automobile and on foot.

From a hard curve on State Route 2, 5.5 miles west of the entrance to the Ottawa Refuge, Bono Road provides access. Like Crane Creek/Magee Marsh, this road too is a drive to Lake Erie and is lined on the west by Ward's Canal, a fishing and boating channel with a public boat ramp, and Metzger Marsh to the east. Roadside parking areas provide places to pull over and observe the marsh and its waterfowl, and spring migration in particular finds plenty of birdwatchers peering through high-powered spotting scopes along here.

The road ends at the lake and a good-sized parking lot. From the mouth of the canal a concrete fishing pier extends out into Lake Erie. Along the south and east side of the parking lot is a small woodland that at times teems with songbirds during spring migration. And to the east along the lakeshore is a dike that keeps Lake Erie at bay and allows the water levels in Metzger to be managed.

There was a previous dike along here when the area that is now the marsh was known as Metzger Farms, a drained area that was a very productive truck farm complete with houses and outbuildings. But in 1929 a storm overwhelmed the dike and Lake Erie reclaimed the land, the Metzger Dike meeting the same fate as virtually all the early dikes that were built along the southwestern Lake Erie shore.

The current stout, stone dike was completed in 1995 and now provides an elevated hike with Lake Erie on one side and Metzger Marsh on the other. The view into the marsh from the dike gives the opportunity to appreciate both its open waters and marshland areas. Great numbers of waterfowl pass through Metzger during the migratory seasons. Even white pelicans, whose range is well west of the Mississippi River, stop in from time to time. And resident bald eagles from the adjacent Ottawa National Wildlife Refuge regularly swoop over the marsh looking for food.

Phragmites, which grow to a height of twelve feet, provide a grassy wall along the marsh boardwalk at Maumee Bay State Park.

The hike along the dike goes for a mile or so to the boundary of the Ottawa Refuge where signs advise that refuge entry from that point is prohibited.

MAUMEE BAY STATE PARK

At Maumee Bay State Park it's possible to take a nearly two-mile marsh walk without your feet ever touching the earth. That's because a long, elevated boardwalk, an impressive effort completed in 1992, winds through acres of wetland. Here the marsh visitor can meander by a variety of wetland habitat as well as a diversity of plant and animal life.

The boardwalk, with both a quarter-mile loop and one-mile loop, starts at the Trautman Nature Center with interpretive signs along the way to enhance the journey. The trail passes through darkening stands of wet woods and bright, open areas of grasses and shrubs. Stands of tall grass, well over head high, wave to and fro on a breezy August day. The tall grasses are called phragmites and grow to a height of twelve feet. The gracefulness of its swaying and bending in the breeze belies the fact that it is a nuisance plant, one that grows thick and chokes out almost every other plant, and brings no food value to the marsh table.

The trail winds along and at its far, eastern end a spur leads off to an observation blind, a small structure with viewing slots cut at various levels to quietly observe the wildlife of the marsh. A bit further on another spur leads to an observation deck, a sea of phragmites lining the way. From the deck can be seen the waters of Lake Erie and in the distant north can be seen the Michigan shoreline, cloaked in a slight blue haze.

As the trail heads back toward the nature center it glides through a stand of buttonbush whose blossoms resemble small, white pincushions and whose nectar draws bumblebees and butterflies. And at the Trautman Nature Center the boardwalk traveler can rest a bit and enjoy attractions that include a display on the Great Black Swamp and a large window on wildlife overlooking a pond.

Maumee Bay State Park is located at Cedar Point and North Curtice roads in eastern Lucas County. In addition to the marsh and boardwalk, the state park offers a range of recreational opportunities, including swimming, fishing, boating camping, lodging, and golf. For more information call the park at 419–836–7758 or the nature center at 419–836–9117.

Lake Erie and the Michigan shore can be seen from the observation deck of the marsh boardwalk at Maumee Bay State Park.

CHAPTER V

MAUMEE RIVER RAMBLE

*I*T BEGINS AT AN HISTORIC, GRACEFUL RAILWAY BRIDGE AND ENDS WELL UPRIVER AT A DAM BUILT IN 1838. A CONTINUOUS RIVER TRAIL THAT TRAVELS THE MAUMEE'S NORTHERN BANK BETWEEN WATERVILLE AND GRAND RAPIDS, OHIO IS AN APPROXIMATELY TEN-MILE TOUR THROUGH NATURE AND HISTORY. ALONG ITS COURSE LAY SWEEPING VIEWS OF THE MAUMEE RIVER AND ITS FLOODPLAINS, DARKENING CANOPIES OF TREES, THE BED WHERE ONCE FLOWED THE MIAMI AND ERIE CANAL, AND SEVERAL METROPARKS OF THE TOLEDO AREA, INCLUDING ONE REACHED ONLY BY FOOT OR BICYCLE.

In what could be called northwest Ohio's "skinniest" park, the Metroparks trail and park system between Waterville and Grand Rapids stretches almost entirely along the former Miami and Erie Canal. The old towpath provides most of the trail surface. Its downriver starting point is at Farnsworth Metropark just south of Waterville where the Bridge Overlook provides a panoramic view of the graceful arches of the old Waterville Electric Bridge and the great rock, Roche de Boeuf, that anchors it center span. Long a favorite of photographers and painters, the bridge and rock with river rapids below might be the most scenic spot on the entire Maumee River.

A sign welcomes visitors to Bend View Metropark, a park accessible only by foot or bicycle.

Through Farnsworth, the River Trail (red) travels about 1.5 miles, passing by handsome, Depression-era shelterhouses built by the WPA and picnic and playgrounds to a boat launch area. Here the red trail ends and the 8.3–mile Towpath Trail (blue) begins. The trail follows the actual towpath of the former Miami and Erie Canal.

The crushed gravel trail, which provides a smooth ride for the bicyclist, leaves Farnsworth behind. The old towpath travels along the remnants of the canal on the right, now a low, damp swale, while on the left side of the trail the Maumee River appears and reappears as it winds its way northeast.

The canopy of trees overhead is dense and the trail is deeply shaded on a late June day. Sycamores, cottonwoods, hickories, hackberries and basswoods all contribute to the lofty, leafy ceiling. The calls of orioles, wood thrushes, Carolina wrens and indigo buntings resonate from overhead while the rich, damp soils of river and canal bottomlands scent the air.

Just over two miles from Farnsworth, the Towpath Trail arrives at what is a bit of serendipity for the first time visitor, Bend View/Canal Lands Metropark, a park with no parking lot. This tiny park, accessible only by the trail, is a little jewel. An overlook provides a sweeping view of the Maumee River where it makes a nearly 90 degree bend and from which the park draws its name. A stout, stone 1941 shelterhouse with a high, beamed ceiling and fireplaces at each end anchors the overlook and a drink of water the old-fashioned way is available from a pump nearby.

Bend View offers solitude and the feeling of being truly off the beaten path. Over time many others must have viewed the river from here. Perhaps Native Americans saw the early fur trappers in their canoes rounding the great bend, little realizing they were harbingers of what would be for them unimaginable change.

The trail continues and about 0.5 miles south of Bend View, a road leads down to the river and a small boat launch area. Here islands of grass rise from the water and dance in the breeze. Great blue herons and great egrets mingle among the

An old shelterhouse built by the Works Progress Administration and a drink of water the old-fashioned way are available at Bend View Metropark.

grassy isles, studies in stillness as they wait for a fish to pass by. The river's rush over the rocky bed of the Maumee fills the air with the soothing resonance of rapids while on the high, far bank across the river rises the old, stone shelterhouse of Wood County's Otsego Park.

The trail goes on and just beyond the three-mile marker a short road slopes to a riverside meadow. It is a managed meadow, done so by the Metroparks, for the benefit of plant and animal life. Wide pathways of mowed grass course through the meadow providing a close view of the various grasses and wildflowers growing there.

From the meadow access on to Grand Rapids, the Towpath Trail is no longer paved with gravel and for the next five miles those traveling by bicycle would surely want to be riding a mountain or trail bike. In addition, a Metroparks sign here advises that from this point on biking is prohibited in wet conditions.

The trail continues and the canopy of trees overhead remains thick, keeping the trail in continuous shade. Other than the call of a bird or the chatter of a squirrel, it's a quiet world, one that gives little clue to the days when the Miami and Erie was a working canal, its peak days about 150 years ago. Back then dozens of canal boats, both passenger and freight, plied their way between Cincinnati and Toledo. The clip-clop of the hooves of the mules towing the boats and the conversations of passengers lounging on deck once echoed here. The boat crews, a generally hard-drinking, hard-swearing lot, added their own unique sounds as well.

At about the six-mile marker the old canal starts to become more defined, with water flowing along the bottom and here kingfishers, herons, and egrets find haven. Before long a sign welcomes trail travelers to Providence Metropark and its 407 acres and shortly beyond that the reconstructed portion of the canal begins. Here the canal of the imagination becomes one of reality as the rebuilt waterway comes complete with a working canal boat and lock.

*P*rovidence Dam in Providence Metropark stretches across the Maumee River. The dam was first built in 1838.

The trail proceeds to Lock # 44 (220 miles to Cincinnati and 30 miles to Toledo) and the Isaac Ludwig Mill built in 1846, now restored and operated by the Metroparks. A replica general store with a gift shop is here as well and harkens to the days when the brawling canal town of Providence marked this spot.

From the lock the trail goes on, ending shortly at Providence Dam, originally built in 1838 and rebuilt a couple of times since then. The water glistens as it rushes over the dam and swirls around the trunks of dead trees borne downriver by floodwaters and grabbed by the dam wall. A two-story stone shelterhouse overlooks the scene and many of the tall cottonwoods growing along the riverbank bear the scars of ice jams past.

Farnsworth, Bend View/Canal Lands and Providence Metroparks are open 7 A.M. until dark year-round and the river trail can be used for cross country skiing. Full restroom facilities are available at Farnsworth and Providence while Bend View has vault toilets and a pump for drinking water. All the parks have reservable, riverside shelterhouses as well. For more information call Farnsworth Metropark at 419–878–7641.

From Farnsworth Metropark, the graceful arches of the former Ohio Electric Interurban Railway Bridge can be seen.

The shelterhouse at Bend View sits above a nearly 90-degree bend in the Maumee River.

HE HOWARD COLLIER AND SPRINGVILLE MARSH STATE NATURE PRESERVES ARE TUCKED DEEP IN THE CORNER OF SOUTH-WESTERN SENECA COUNTY AND ARE ONLY ABOUT A HALF DOZEN OR SO MILES APART AS THE CROW FLIES. BOTH OFFER QUIET RESPITE WELL OFF THE BEATEN PATH AND BOTH ARE PART OF THE STATE NATURE PRESERVE SYSTEM. OTHER THAN THAT THEY HAVE LITTLE IN COMMON.

HOWARD COLLIER STATE NATURE PRESERVE

It's obvious at the beginning to the first-time time visitor to Howard Collier State Nature Preserve that he or she is someplace special. From the upper parking area a spectacular stairway, nearly 100 steps, winds and falls dramatically down a deeply wooded hillside to the floodplain of the Sandusky River. Such a scene might be common to the hills of southern Ohio but certainly is an anomaly in the flatlands that characterize most of the northwestern part of the state.

From the top of the stairs the one-mile Beech Ridge Trail courses along a sharp ridge before dropping down to the floodplain below. Through the hushed world of the floodplain, the trail tracks along the Sandusky River, a designated state scenic

A wooden stairway of nearly 100 steps descends down a hillside to the Sandusky River valley floor at Howard Collier State Nature Preserve.

river, sheltered by a canopy of sycamore, oak, ash, cottonwood, and tuliptrees. Nourished by the river and its rich bottomland, many of the mature trees are of old-growth height.

The trail eventually winds back to the foot of the stairs through bottomland that lights up in a floral display every spring. Dutchman's breeches, white yellow trout-lily, squirrel corn, sharp-lobed hepatica and three species of trillium, including the state wildflower, the large flowered trillium, are among the flowers found here in May.

The floodplain can also be accessed directly via the Little Fox Run Trail, which leaves from the lower parking area. This roughly half-mile trail passes through an area of both mature forest and reverting farm field. Sections of board-walk cross the wetter areas.

The Howard Collier State Nature Preserve is located in southwest Seneca County three miles northeast of the village of McCutchenville. From State Route 53 in McCutchenville go three miles east on County Road 58 then 0.5 miles north on Township Road 131. Proceed then 0.25 miles east on Township Road 38. The preserve has a large parking area, no other facilities.

SPRINGVILLE MARSH STATE NATURE PRESERVE

Springville Marsh State Nature Preserve gives little indication of the rather rough treatment accorded it by humans in the past. For the marsh was once ditched, drained, burned, farmed and even mined.

The marsh at one time was part of a much larger wetland called Big Spring Prairie that stretched across much of western Seneca County. Too wet for agriculture, it was avoided by the early settlers and was given in 1818 by the U.S. government to Wyandot Indians for hunting and trapping. Once the Indians were exiled west, Big Spring Prairie was slowly drained into farm and pasture land. Train tracks

White trillium light up the valley floor in the spring at Howard Collier State Nature Preserve.

were laid across it, sparks from the locomotives starting fires at times during the dry months, and in the fall dried fields were burned to make next year's mowing easier.

In the early 1900s, the area where Springville Marsh is now was primarily an onion farm. Then in 1937 an agricultural chemical company bought the land and turned it into a "muck" mine. The calcium-rich soil of the marsh, or muck, was used in the manufacture of fertilizer and two engines and a dozen rail cars were used to haul the fertile earth out of the marsh. Mining was ended in 1956 and fund-raising by concerned citizens in the late 1970s led to the purchase of the 161–acre parcel and eventual transfer to the state in 1981.

Springville Marsh today is living evidence of the remarkable ability of nature not only to heal itself but to prosper. Lush cattail marshes and sedge meadows flourish here along with Canadian and Atlantic coastal plain plant species that date to the ice age, all nourished by calcium-rich springs of the marsh. Several species of fern and small orchids grow here along with other species of wildflowers and a sharp-eyed visitor might see a rare spotted turtle that makes its home here.

Over 2,600 feet of boardwalk in the northern part of the preserve winds through both open marsh and islands of trees. There's both a bird observation blind and a ten-foot high viewing platform which gives a fine view of a tall cattail marsh and pond. Interpretive signs posted at intervals along the boardwalk serve to enhance the journey.

Springville Marsh State Nature Preserve is located in Seneca County about four miles north of the town of Carey on Township Road 24, one mile west of U.S. 23/ State Route 199. The marsh has a small parking area with informational displays, no other facilities. The boardwalk has no kick rails thus it is recommended that wheelchair users not use the trail alone.

A cattail marsh pond is one of the features of Springville Marsh State Nature Preserve

CHAPTER VII

FULTON COUNTY FORESTS

𝒯HE ONCE SWAMPY SOILS OF FULTON COUNTY HAVE LONG BEEN DRAINED AND CLEARED OF TREES. MOST OF THE COUNTY NOW IS AN EMERALD PATCHWORK OF AGRICULTURAL FIELDS YIELDING HEALTHY CROPS OF CORN, WHEAT AND SOYBEANS YEAR AFTER YEAR. HOWEVER, IN THE WESTERN REACHES OF THE COUNTY TWO ISLANDS OF WOODLAND GREEN RISE FROM THE FARM FIELDS, ONE ANCIENT AND THE OTHER OF A MORE RECENT VINTAGE.

GOLL WOODS STATE NATURE PRESERVE

Roget's Thesaurus lists thirty-one synonyms for the word "majestic" and all of them would apply to the old-growth oak trees of Goll Woods in Fulton County, the 1960s-era term "mind-blowing" included. Massive bur oaks, some believed to be over 300 years old, tower towards the clouds here. What really staggers the imagination when looking at these giants is realizing that such trees covered most of northwest Ohio when the settlers, including a young couple named Peter and Catherine Goll, first arrived.

The year was 1836 when the Golls ended their long, tiring journey from France and settled in a Fulton County wilderness

The old growth oak trees at Goll Woods State Nature Preserve dwarf human beings, especially small ones. (The author thanks his niece Nora Mollenkopf for her able assistance.)

to chase their American dream. What greeted them was a dense, wet woodlands that needed to be cleared before crops could be planted. However, the Golls were different. Unlike virtually all the other pioneers to the region at the time, they saved a portion of their forest, seeing a sublime beauty where perhaps others might only see financial opportunity.

Although their farm eventually grew to over 600 acres, they, and succeeding generations of Golls, carefully guarded their "Big Woods" from what had to be the persistent and lucrative offers of timber operators. In 1966 the state purchased the land from great-granddaughter Florence Goll Louys and her children and the Goll Woods State Nature Preserve was born.

Goll Woods today is approximately 100 acres of old woodland and over 200 acres of younger forest for a total of 321. Four trails ranging from one to 1.75 miles wind through both areas with the Bur Oak and Cottonwood Trails providing entrance to what is a rarity not only in Ohio, but in most areas east of the Mississippi: an essentially undisturbed stand of old-growth timber.

The old woods features fine specimens of such trees as sugar maple, tuliptree, white ash, white oak, shagbark hickory, cottonwood and basswood. But it is the bur oaks that are the stars of this forest. Many of them are over 100 feet tall, their massive trunks with deeply furrowed bark rising more than fifty feet in the air before the first limb reaches out. Most of the trees were here during the American Revolution; some were here when the pilgrims landed at Plymouth Rock. Virtually all were here when Native Americans still lived in the area and hunted beneath their lofty canopies.

The bur oaks of Goll Woods can also be viewed horizontally since many have been slammed to the ground by windstorms over the years, mostly trees that were weakened by old age and/or disease. The ones that fell across trails have been cut to clear the way and their growth rings can be seen, hundreds of bands of varying width reflecting the good, the fair and the poor years of growth as decreed by nature.

The gnarled limbs of the aged oaks at Goll Woods reach for the sky.

In addition to the bur oaks, the nature preserve, a roughly rectangular-shaped parcel divided in half by a road, features a pine plantation to the north of the old woods and on the west side of the road, more hardwood forest that can be wandered via the Tuliptree and Toadshade Trails. In the northwest part of the preserve is Goll Cemetery, a hilltop burying ground that dates to 1853. Here lie many generations of the Goll family, people whose wisdom and vision have granted northwest Ohio a wooded jewel.

Across from the cemetery a portion of the Toadshade Trail leads along the rich bottomland of the Tiffin River where large beech, sycamore and oak trees ascend. The trail leads to an observation deck on a high bank of the river, an area surrounded by a darkening stand of pure white pine whose soft needles sway and sigh in the wind on a breezy day.

Goll Woods State Nature Preserve is located in Fulton County about 1.5 miles north of Archbold—from State Route 66 go three miles west on Township Road F then 0.25 miles south on Township Road 26 to the main parking lot and trailhead. There is an informational display at the parking lot with guides to the posted Bur Oak and Cottonwood Trails. Goll Woods is also known for its outstanding spring wildflowers. It is a moist woods so "mud shoes" are good idea. The mosquitoes there can be voracious in the summer—the Ohio Department of Natural Resources recommends spring or autumn visitation. The main parking lot has latrines; there is a second parking lot along the Tiffin River off Township Road F. The preserve is open dawn to dusk-year-round. Nearby attractions include Sauder Farm and Village just north of Archbold on State Route 2 , 0.25 miles east of State Route 66.

HARRISON LAKE STATE PARK

About a half dozen miles north of Goll Woods lies Harrison Lake State Park, nearly 250 acres of land and water for recreation and relaxation. In 1941 a dam was built over Mill Creek and Harrison Lake was created. The six-plus decades that have passed since have allowed trees to mature and line its shores and the lake, with the exception of the dam and spillways at its east end, bears little evidence of its man-made origins.

Harrison Lake is a good place to spend a lazy summer or fall afternoon. There's a swimming beach and white pine-shaded picnic ground on a peninsula of land connected to the mainland of the park by a footbridge. Other picnic grounds dot the hilly areas around the lake, several with rustic stone shelterhouses.

The lake is popular with anglers offering catches of largemouth and small-mouth bass, bluegill and crappie. Boats quietly ply the waters of the lake as only non-powered watercraft and boats with electric motors are permitted. For those looking to spend more than an afternoon, Harrison Lake has a campground with nearly 200 sites.

A 3.5–mile hiking trail circles the lake passing through the mature, mixed hardwood forest that has grown along its shore. And at the east end of the lake, water tumbles down the spillway, rushing along as it glistens in the sun, in what may be the closest thing northwest Ohio has to a waterfall.

Harrison Lake State Park is located in western Fulton County on County Road 27, two miles south of U.S. 20, about three miles west of Fayette. The campground has 199 sites, 144 of which have electricity. For more information call the park at 419–237–2593.

An old, stone shelterhouse sits along the shore at Harrison Lake.

The waters of Harrison Lake tumble over the dam and down the spillway.

CHAPTER VIII

WEST TOLEDO WANDERS

W ILDWOOD PRESERVE METROPARK

OF THE JEWELS IN THE CROWN THAT MAKES UP THE METROPARKS OF THE TOLEDO AREA, THE SHINIEST ONE PERHAPS IS WILDWOOD PRESERVE METROPARK, A PARK THAT ALMOST WASN'T. ONCE THE PRIVATE ESTATE OF CHAMPION SPARK PLUG COMPANY CO-FOUNDER ROBERT A. STRANAHAN, PLANS WERE ANNOUNCED IN 1973 BY A LOCAL DEVELOPER TO CONSTRUCT LUXURY HOUSING ON THE LAND, PLANS THAT WOULD HAVE FOREVER DESTROYED ITS NATURAL VALUE. A GRASSROOTS CITIZENS CAMPAIGN WAS STARTED AND, THOUGH GIVEN LITTLE CHANCE INITIALLY, SUCCESSFULLY CONVINCED VOTERS TO APPROVE A SPECIAL PROPERTY TAX LEVY TO FINANCE THE PURCHASE OF THE LAND. ON MEMORIAL DAY 1975, THE PARK WAS OPENED TO THE PUBLIC. IT HAS SINCE BECOME THE METROPARKS' MOST HEAVILY VISITED PROPERTY.

Many natural worlds make up the 493 acres of Wildwood. Deep wooded ravines, mature upland forest, river and valley, floodplain, overlooks, meadows, tallgrass prairie, wildlife, and wildflowers. Some man-made worlds are there as well, including Manor House, the 1938 Georgian Colonial mansion of the estate's former owner, a restored one-room schoolhouse, and a covered, wooden bridge over the Ottawa River. Here are a couple of the worlds of Wildwood.

Snow blankets the Lusk/Mewborn boardwalk in the Ottawa River Valley at Wildwood Preserve.

It is a realm that is literally sunken below the clatter of daily reality, a place darkened by towering trees and hushed by earthen walls. At the bottom of fifty steps that zigzag down behind the mansion at Wildwood Preserve Metropark lies the Ottawa River Valley.

Here the Lusk/Mewborn Boardwalk gives entrance to an infrequently seen world, a river and valley in an urban area in virtually pristine condition. Part of the park's 1.4–mile Floodplain Trail (blue), it is named for two volunteers instrumental in the levy campaign to create the park.

The boardwalk winds for a third of a mile on the Ottawa River's bank, gliding walkers over ground too wet to journey much of the year. In doing so it takes its travelers to the river valley's world, to witness its fertile bottomland, its rich diversity of flora and fauna, and its timeless cycle of the season's change.

When the year begins the valley sleeps, locked in snow and ice and swept by frigid winds. Winter birds, squirrels, and deer forage the frozen floor during the short days and endure the long, cold nights. The thaws and freezes of winter send the river over its banks and pull it back in, leaving the trunks of the floodplain's trees dressed in a delicate, lacy skirt of ice. On snowy days, sound in the valley is muffled while on clear ones, the sun setting against a cold winter sky paints the limbs of the trees in black silhouette. The boardwalk falls quiet for much of the time as an icy coat often makes it a bit treacherous to travel.

Finally the valley emerges from February and into March. The sun returns slowly toward the north from its winter sojourn and the days begin to lengthen. Rains and melting snow bring spring floods, sending water the color of coffee with cream swirling around and under the boardwalk, giving its traveler the eerie feel of walking on water. The floodwaters flatten the floodplain's vegetation, spreading seeds and a nourishing layer of silt.

April sees the first new growth as green shoots poke out of the winter brown ground and from the valley's trees, another season's leaves begin to emerge. The boardwalk vibrates with walkers and runners as the long winter has passed and the soul-restoring first days of spring have arrived.

The Ottawa River flows past the Lusk/Mewborn boardwalk at Wildwood Preserve

May brings wildflowers and warming, lingering, days as the greening of the valley is in full swing. Migrating birds pass through and rumbles of thunder echo from spring storms. June brings the first hot, humid days, giving the moist valley a tropical feel. The soaring ceiling of cottonwood, oak, and sycamore trees are in full leaf by now, their massive trunks rooted deep in the rich, wet earth. Shafts of light are filtered downward and great vines climb most of the trees. Many of the smaller trees in the valley are completely covered with vines, looking like great, green quilts have been tossed over them in this northern version of a rain forest.

Through the summer the songs of birds float through the valley air from nearby brushy growth or float down from high branches above. A rainbow of color streaks by in the crimson blush of a cardinal, the fiery orange of a Baltimore oriole, or the royal blue of an indigo bunting. The grasses and plants growing from the floodplain floor are in their zenith, rising well above the level of the boardwalk. The river, save for some gentle rapids at the foot of the stairs, is in summer somnolence. Brown, barely moving, the footprints of animals are pressed into its soft, muddy banks.

The summer of the year is all too short of course and in September the green of the vale gradually gives way to the colors of autumn's palette, while damp, fall mornings often cloak the valley in a blanket of mist. The rains return, the days grow shorter and the wind sends leaves skittering along the boardwalk. November finds most of the color of the valley muted to copper and rust and a wistful chill hanging in the air. And by December all the leaves are gone, layered in an organic carpet on the floodplain floor to nourish next year's growth, the first snows begin to fall, and the number of boardwalk travelers dwindles.

When the year comes to an end the valley sleeps; locked in snow and ice and swept by frigid winds.

OCTOBER MEADOW

What most would regard as a perfect fall day starts when a large dome of high pressure parks itself off the coast of the Carolinas, its powerful clockwise swirl hurling a blanket

October invites the colors of the season in the trees rimming the meadow at Wildwood Preserve

of warm air north over the Midwest. Temperatures rise, a southern breeze stirs, and an azure blue sky arches over a sunlit autumn land. It is such days that are the epitome of that phenomenon known as Indian Summer. And it is on such days a walk through a meadow, such as the one at Wildwood Preserve, is a reminder of how good life can be.

The 1.2–mile Meadow Trail (yellow) winds through this rolling, grassy and brushy plain. On a perfect October day a warm wind puts the meadow in motion, tall grasses and brush wave and dance while leaves spin through the air like so much colored confetti. The soft autumn tans of the meadow grasses reach to the tall maple, sassafras, and tuliptrees rimming the perimeter, ablaze in red and gold October flame.

To the north and east the meadow slopes gently down toward the Ottawa River and at the top of this slope stands the lord of this grassland; a massive white oak tree that dates to well before the Civil War. The tree's great trunk rises in the air and its thick and muscular branches build an immense crown high against a deep blue sky. The leaves, transformed from summertime green to bronze, sigh and rattle in a strong gust of wind.

The sun is on its annual journey toward the southern hemisphere and its warm rays are soft, unlike the harsher, burning rays of summer. They slant in at a low angle, stretching shadows across the land. A hawk circles lazily overhead while a few bees buzz and an occasional monarch butterfly flutters past, tardy in its migration to Mexico.

Migrating about the meadow too are people, the sun warming their faces and the wind tousling their hair. They move about slowly, in no hurry at all, knowing how special and infrequent such Indian Summer days are, days to be relished and not rushed.

All good things come to an end, the saying goes, and so, too this weather cannot last. A storm system building in the Canadian prairies will arrive before long and a damp, chill wind will sweep from a gray sky. But until then the glory of this autumn meadow will continue to showcase summer's spectacular exit.

Wildwood Preserve Metropark is located at 5100 W. Central Avenue in Toledo, 0.5 milse east of Reynolds Road, and is open daily 7 A.M. to dark. In addition to five walking trails and a paved all-purpose trail, the park provides access to the 6.3–mile paved University/Parks Trail. The Manor House is open for tours noon to 5 P.M. Wednesday through Sunday. For more information call the park at 419–535–3058.

A mighty white oak tree dominates the meadow at Wildwood Preserve.

From the first crocus that pushes its way up through the cold March soil to delicate dahlias, brilliant right up to the first frosts of autumn, Toledo Botanical Garden blooms, blossoms, burgeons, and brightens.

Toledo Botanical Garden is a collection of many gardens; of flowering annuals and perennials, bushes and trees, of vegetables, herbs, hostas, and grasses. However, it is also home to stately oak and sycamore trees, quiet ponds, public sculptures, resident artist groups, a lithophane museum and an 1837 pioneer homestead. Tucked a bit of out of sight in a residential neighborhood, the sixty-acre garden has been at times called "Toledo's best kept secret," making it a place where not only beauty but a bit of solitude might be found in an urban environment.

Along the Garden's northern edge is a five-acre shade garden where lofty oaks shadow the ground below and ferns and hostas flourish. The hosta collection here has been recognized as a National Display Garden by the American Hosta Society and forms a literal "hosta river" that flows under a footbridge.

Also in the shade garden are two gazebos, one along a small pond where water lilies float on lazy summer days. Azaleas and rhododendrons also abound here and light up the grounds every spring. And a wintertime walker in these woods could take in Robert Frost's "Stopping by Woods on a Snowy Evening" mounted on a post, one of a number of poems with a theme of trees or "poet trees" placed around the Garden.

South from the conference center, sycamore trees escort the path through Sycamore Allee, trees lanky and leaning ever so slightly. In summer their smooth, chalky bark peels off in large flakes exposing green and brown layers underneath and giving the appearance of dappled sunlight. In winter the bark is almost stark white, especially against an arctic blue sky. Native Americans once called them "ghost trees."

From the sycamores the path winds around "Monument to a Tree," one of the Garden's public sculptures, and descends to Crosby Lake, named for George Crosby,

A gazebo overlooks a pond in the shade garden at Toledo Botanical Garden.

whose donation of land led to Crosby Park in 1964, which eventually grew into Toledo Botanical Garden. Rising above the lake stands a tall European larch tree, a deciduous pine, whose feathery green needles turn bright yellow in the autumn before falling. Several more larches dot an island in the lake. Flocks of migrating Canada geese alight on the water in the late fall and early winter and again in the spring when the ice melts, to rest and feed before moving on. At times there are hundreds of them here.

An arched bridge with the rush of a waterfall underneath crosses over to the south side of the lake and here brick pathways wind through a variety of gardens, including a cottage garden marked by an artisan-crafted stone wall with windows and wrought iron gate. On a plain above the south side of the lake is Grand Allee, double rows of sterling silver linden trees lining parallel pathways.

Back over the bridge the path climbs past the dahlia garden and to the Peter Navarre cabin, built by the son of one of Toledo's earliest pioneers. Adjacent to the cabin is a pioneer vegetable garden where produce and flowers common to the nineteenth century are grown. Behind the cabin and across the lane is the administration building. On its east side is a rose garden with over 200 varieties of roses while on its west is a modern vegetable garden where seeds of new hybrids sprout.

From the administration building spreads a resident artist village, where fruits of the mind flourish. The buildings here house pottery, glass, painting, photography, and weaving clubs. Also here is the Blair Lithophane Museum, a collection of pictures made of delicate porcelain, an art popular in the nineteenth century.

Toledo Botanical Garden, located on Elmer Drive in western Toledo between Reynolds Road and Holland-Sylvania Avenue, is open year-round with seasonal hours posted on the gate. Admission is free except during special events, which include the Crosby Festival for the Arts, Ohio's oldest juried outdoor art show, in late June. For more information call the garden at 419–936–2986.

Canada geese and a pair of mute swans find open water on Toledo Botanical Garden's Crosby Lake.

Sycamore trees line a path along Sycamore Allee on a summer morning at Toledo Botanical Garden.

A window frames a floral scene in Toledo Botanical Garden's cottage garden.

An 1837 pioneer homestead, originally built in East Toledo, finds a home at Toledo Botanical Garden.

CHAPTER IX

LAKE LA SU AN WILDLIFE AREA

ESTLED IN THE FAR, FAR NORTHWEST CORNER OF NORTH WEST OHIO LIES A SCENE MORE REMINISCENT OF NEW ENGLAND THAN OF THIS PART OF THE BUCKEYE STATE, LAKE LA SU AN WILDLIFE AREA, ACRES OF ROLLING WOODLAND, FIELDS AND WETLANDS. FOURTEEN LAKES AND PONDS GRACE THE AREA AS WELL, MAKING IT A FISHERMEN'S AND WILDLIFE LOVERS' DESTINATION.

The largest of the lakes is La Su An, a rambling, eighty-two-acre body of water with a bit of history to it. According to an early landowner, the lake originally was about six acres resting in a deep muck pocket, its shore boggy and dense with standing and fallen trees. Then known as Hays Lake, it lay sleepy and undisturbed over the decades, a good enough fishing pond until a stream deepening project allowed an invasion of carp which ended the lake's angling allure.

Then in the late 1950s a man named Edward Brodbeck acquired the lake and surrounding area. He had a vision for the water and land and, doing most of the work himself, set about building dams, clearing excess brush and trees, digging additional small lakes and ponds, and laying roads in the elevated areas. In the process he increased Hays Lake in size over tenfold.

H ills hide a quiet pond at Lake La Su An Wildlife Area.

His efforts were at times viewed with a skeptical eye by some local observers. However, he continued to chase his dream, which by the late 1960s resulted in an over 500–acre recreational area and retreat which he named, appropriately, Dreamland Acres. He opened up the complex to area residents who, for a small fee, could take advantage of its outstanding fishing. In addition, he opened the roads in the autumn for fall color drives.

In 1978, getting up in years, he told a local newspaper, "God has sent me here to do something with this land and I hope it can be saved." In 1981 the state of Ohio did just that when it began acquisition of the area which has now grown to over 2,000 acres, the centerpiece of which is Lake La Su An. And around the lake is a gravel access road that provides a good hiking path. The road, roughly 2.5 miles, leaves west from the main parking lot and fish check station and rolls north through meadows and cropland a bit before dropping downhill into thick woods and across a low earthen dam.

Here sits a pond, hidden by wooded hills, its surface emerald green in summertime attire. From the water a battalion of dead trees rise tall in the air, barren of growth but not of life. Red-headed woodpeckers call the trees home, their scarlet crowns brilliant as they dash from tree to tree. Brilliant too is the uncommonly seen prothonotary warbler, a spring/early summer nester here, and a flash of pure gold on a sunny day. It's easy to see why it was once called the golden swamp warbler. In sizable contrast to the tiny warbler, black crowned night herons, and at times their huge cousins, the great blue heron, crouch in the branches, studies in stillness before taking wing. Also blue but iridescently so is the occasional indigo bunting passing through.

From this bit of secluded serenity the road continues along the west side of the lake, climbing again and coursing along a ridge shaded by a dense beech-maple-oak forest. Not too long after passing Lou's Pond the road winds around the northern end of the lake and to its eastern side, one dominated by fields and meadows. Here grassland-loving birds such as meadowlarks and bobolinks might be seen. From the

Trees in autumn glory reach to the shore at Lake La Su An Wildlife Area.

open, hilly areas on the eastern side a panoramic lake view sweeps before the eyes, one uncommon in the flatness that characterizes most of northwest Ohio. And the lucky birdwatcher here might see an osprey soaring high over the lake ready to execute a spectacular dive to the water, flying away with a fish wriggling in its talons.

The road continues, passing by Ed's Pond and to the south side of the lake and back to the parking lot and fish check station. Although it's been a long time since the area has been called Dreamland Acres, Edward Brodbeck's dream is alive and well.

Lake La Su An Wildlife Area is located in Williams County on County Road R, six miles west of Pioneer, Ohio. There is a large parking area at the fish check station and maps of the wildlife area are available at the station. The area's fourteen lakes and ponds are known for good largemouth bass and bluegill fishing; fishing is by permit only. For more information call the fish check station at 419–636–6189 or the wildlife area manager at 419–485–9092.

CHAPTER X

OTSEGO PARK

𝒜T ONLY TEN ACRES, WOOD COUNTY'S OTSEGO PARK MAY
BE ONE OF THE SMALLER PARKS AROUND BUT IN THE
CATEGORY OF SCENIC VIEW, IT'S VERY LARGE. THE CENTERPIECE OF
THE PARK IS AN OLD SHELTERHOUSE CALLED OTSEGO STONE
HALL THAT'S PERCHED ON A HIGH BANK OF THE MAUMEE RIVER.
FROM HERE STRETCHES A SWEEPING VISTA OF THE MAUMEE
RIVER, PERHAPS THE FINEST VIEW FOUND ON THE WATERWAY'S EN-
TIRE 100–MILE COURSE.

From the back patio and porch of the hall the river and its
various seasonal moods can be seen and savored. The view is excellent from inside as well, as connected to the stone hall is an indoor overlook with bay windows providing a panorama. Nature
and wildlife exhibits in glass display cases and on the walls add to
the indoor experience.

The river bottom below is studded with rocks and boulders
and the water swirls and eddies on its journey to Lake Erie. The
roar of rapids rolls up the high riverbank and over the hall, blan-
keting the small park in a soothing refrain. Stairs descend to water's edge where the rapids glisten on a sunny day and the park's
four small islands can be seen. Among rock and isle, herons and

Rapids ripple the Maumee River below Otsego Park.

egrets stand on spindly legs while small flocks of lake gulls bob along the river's surface, seeming to have not a care in the world.

Otsego Park is located on State Route 65 at the intersection of State Route 235, about five miles downriver from Grand Rapids, Ohio. The indoor overlook is open daily until dark. The park has picnic tables, grills restrooms and offers river fishing and canoe access. For more information call the Wood County Park District at 419–353–1897 or 800–321–1897.

An indoor overlook at Otsego Park offers a panoramic view of the Maumee River.

CHAPTER XI

MARBLEHEAD'S FLOWER AND TOWER

*L*AKESIDE DAISY STATE NATURE PRESERVE

THE PROCESS OF ROCK QUARRYING IS, BY ITS VERY NATURE, A DESTRUCTIVE ONE. THE GROUND IS BLASTED, GOUGED AND SCRAPED, DESTROYING ALL VEGETATION AND LEAVING BEHIND A BLEAK, LIFELESS LANDSCAPE. THE LIMESTONE QUARRIES ON THE MARBLEHEAD PENINSULA, WHERE QUARRYING HAS TAKEN PLACE SINCE THE MID-1800S, ARE NO DIFFERENT.

Rising like a Phoenix from the ashes, however, on former quarry land in Marblehead is the Lakeside daisy, a yellow wildflower shining from rock and scrub. Each May the daisy makes its brilliant but brief appearance, Marblehead being home to the only natural population of the flower in the United States and one of only three such locales in all of North America. The flower is listed as both state endangered and federally threatened.

The daisy blooms in early May on a leafless stalk, usually 6–11 inches tall. They bloom virtually at the same time transforming a barren, sun-baked landscape into a floral showpiece. Their color begins to fade after a week or so and by the second half of May, generally, the show is over. But their annual appear-

The Marblehead peninsula is one of only three places in North America where the rare Lakeside daisy blooms.

ance serves as a reminder that even under mankind's heavy hand nature has a way of somehow persevering.

The nineteen-acre preserve was created in 1988 and is named for Colleen Taylor and Ruth Fiscus, two women who were instrumental in gaining protection of the site. It is open to the public during the month of May only, with a permit being required the rest of the year.

Lakeside Daisy State Nature Preserve is located on Alexander Pike which runs south from West Main Street in downtown Marblehead. There is a small parking area with an informational display, no other facilities.

MARBLEHEAD LIGHTHOUSE STATE PARK

When it comes to size in relation to other state parks, Marblehead Lighthouse weighs in at a comparatively tiny nine acres. And although it is one of Ohio's newest state parks it just may be its oldest in terms of history, as Marblehead's life-saving beacon has been piercing the Lake Erie night here for over 180 years.

Lighthouses, which date to well before the time of Christ, have long captured the human imagination and fascination and Marblehead is no exception. Marblehead is one of the most popular and heavily photographed lighthouses on all of the Great Lakes.

There were only twenty-three states in the Union in 1822 when the light's first keeper, Benajah Wolcott, made his initial trip up the steps to light the lamps of the lighthouse. Benajah faithfully lit those whale oil lamps for ten years before falling victim to a cholera epidemic. His wife Rachel then assumed the duties, becoming the first female lighthouse keeper on the Great Lakes, a trust she carried out for twenty-two years. Over the years human lighthouse keepers went the way of whale oil lamps and now an automated system beams a green signal out over the lake every six seconds.

A frozen January morning finds the Marblehead light locked in ice.

The lighthouse was built with native limestone and its walls are five feet thick at the base, and narrow to two feet at the top. Topping off at eighty-five feet, its gleaming white tower and red railing and cap are a study in elegant simplicity. The light sits on the rocky tip of the Marblehead Peninsula and on the shore below it, great slabs of limestone outcropping keep the lake at bay. The waves crashing over the rocks on a breezy day is a scene more reminiscent of the coast of Maine than of Lake Erie. And on a frozen winter's day the icebound rocky tip and lighthouse offer a scene serene to the point of being surreal.

The grounds around the lighthouse offer waterside picnicking and fine views of Lake Erie, Sandusky Bay and both Kelley's and South Bass islands. The 352–foot tall granite column of the Perry's Victory and International Peace Memorial easily landmarks the latter. Across from the lighthouse is the Keeper's House, inside of which is a museum operated by the Marblehead Lighthouse Historical Society which is open for tours when the tower is open.

Marblehead Lighthouse State Park is located in Marblehead, Ohio at the eastern end of town. The tower is open for tours weekday afternoons June 1 through the Friday before Labor Day; check for current times. For more information call East Harbor State Park at 419–734–4424. The original Keeper's House, also known as the Wolcott House and built by Benajah Wolcott in 1822, is located at 9999 Bayshore Road on the south side of Marblehead Peninsula about 2.5 miles beyond the lighthouse. The handsome, stone house, restored by the Ottawa County Historical Society, is the oldest structure in Ottawa County and one of the oldest in all of northwest Ohio and is open for tours daily during the summer months. For more information call the Keeper's House at 419–798–9339.

A gull flies by as waves wash over the rocks below the Marblehead Lighthouse.

CHAPTER XII

RIVERSIDE RIDE

*G*OING FOR A SUNDAY DRIVE IS AN AMERICAN TRADITION AND PERHAPS THE PRETTIEST SUCH DRIVE IN NORTHWEST OHIO LIES ON STATE ROUTE 424 BETWEEN THE MAUMEE RIVER CITIES OF NAPOLEON AND DEFIANCE, OHIO THE ROUTE, DESIGNATED BY THE STATE AS A SCENIC ROUTE/OHIO BYWAY, WAS ONCE VOTED IN A SURVEY SPONSORED BY THE MOTORCYCLE MANUFACTURER HARLEY-DAVIDSON AS ONE OF THE TEN BEST TOURING ROADS IN THE UNITED STATES.

The route leaves downtown Napoleon below the massive and majestic Henry County courthouse and is escorted out of town by several riverside parks. Before long the remnants of the Miami and Erie Canal and its clearly defined towpath appear as the road winds pleasantly along, rolling past river, woods and field, and through the quiet hamlet of Florida, established in 1834 where once stood the Indian village of Snaketown.

A few miles beyond Florida the appearance of picnic tables signals the beginning of Independence Dam State Park, a three-mile-long recreational area stretched along a spit of land between the former canal and the Maumee River. Lock #13 of the Miami

The month of May brings out the soft greens of spring at Independence Dam State Park.

and Erie Canal marks the entrance to the state park where canal boats, or packets, once squeezed through the lock's narrow limestone walls.

The park offers plenty of quiet, riverside picnicking along with several miles of park road for walking, hiking or biking. The sound of the Maumee River rushing over Independence Dam fills the air here and a slight current of water still moves along the old canal bottom even though its transportation heyday sailed into history long ago.

State Route 424 continues and beyond the state park the canal disappears and the road hugs the bank of the Maumee River. It rolls through Independence, a once thriving canal town, and into Defiance and the confluence of the Maumee and Auglaize rivers. When General "Mad Anthony" Wayne came here in 1794, the bark cabins and cultivated fields of Indians lined both sides of the rivers. Now Pontiac Park graces the river here, named for the legendary Ottawa chief who was believed to have been born here in 1712 and who led a 1763 rebellion against the British. Numerous historical markers dot the park, including one to a great apple tree that once grew here, the largest on record, and one that bore 200 bushels of apples in a single year.

Across Maumee River from the park rises an impressive bluff. It was on this bluff that Anthony Wayne built Fort Defiance proclaiming, "I defy the English, the Indians, and all the devils in Hell to take it." And it was from here he marched to the Battle of Fallen Timbers which forever changed the history of the area. Now this most decidedly peaceful promontory provides a fine view of two rivers joining to become one.

State Route 424 between Napoleon and Defiance is approximately fourteen miles in length. Independence Dam State park offers riverside hiking and picnicking as well as boating, canoeing, and fishing.

The Maumee River flows around an island at Independence Dam State Park.

FRENCH INDIAN
APPLE TREE
LARGEST ON RECORD
9 FT. DIAMETER
60 FT SPREAD 35 HIGH
BORE 200 BU. 1872
1670 — 1887

A stone marker in Pontiac Park recalls the largest apple tree on record that once stood there.

A bluff above the confluence of the Maumee and Auglaize rivers marks the spot where Fort Defiance once stood.

ABOUT THE AUTHOR

Jim Mollenkopf is a Toledo, Ohio author and photographer. A former social worker then newspaper reporter, this is his fifth book. He previously wrote and published:

Lake Erie Sojourn: an autumn tour of the parks, public places, and history of the lake erie shore

The Great Black Swamp; historical tales of 19th century northwest ohio

The Great Black Swamp II: more historical tales of northwest ohio

Civil War Stories of Northwest Ohio Heroes